D0815261

The God-Illuminated Cook

The God-Illuminated Cook

a new edition of
The Practice of the Presence of God

by Brother Lawrence

Edited by Robin Dawes and
the Editors of 24 Magazine

ᄔ

LIFESAVERS LIBRARY
A Division of East Ridge Press
Callicoon, N.Y. 12723 U.S.A.

First Edition 1975
Second Edition 1979

Library of Congress catalog card number 74-84399
ISBN: 0-914896-00-8

Publisher's Note

We are bookmakers who specialize in the literature of the lifesavers way of life (see page 131). It needs saying that in the pursuit of this way — based on the Way of ways — books can be well used or abused. Reading is helpful, and indeed necessary, but it is no substitute for *doing the work* of the Way in obedience to the will of God.

Hear what a great master of the spiritual life (Caussade) says:

"The divine influence alone can sanctify us. . . . Without it reading only darkens the mind. . . . All reading not intended for us by God is dangerous. It is by doing the will of God and obeying his holy inspirations that we obtain grace, and this grace works in our hearts, through our reading or any other employment. Apart from God, reading is empty and vain and, being deprived for us of the life-giving power of the action of God, only succeeds in emptying the heart by the very fullness it gives to the mind.

"This divine will, working in the soul of a simple ignorant girl by means of sufferings and actions of a very ordinary nature, produces a state of supernatural life without the mind being filled with self-exalting ideas; whereas the proud man who studies spiritual books merely out of curiosity receives no more than the dead letter into his mind, and, the will of God having no connection with his reading, his heart becomes ever harder and more withered."

The illustrations of this book are of Celtic and Pictish origin.* Many of them are taken from the *Book of Kells*, an eighth century illuminated manuscript of the Latin Gospels. Each of these medieval figures is a *mandala*, a design organized around a center from which holy power emanates, a universal symbol of the Self—the Christ within—the presence of God in man.

* From *Celtic Art*, by George Bain. 1973: Dover. Originally published in Scotland by William Maclellan.

This book is designed to enable and to facilitate *meditative reading* according to the suggestions of Bernard of Clairvaux and other masters of prayer, i.e., quiet, unhurried reading with intervals of meditation. Each spread in the book presents to the reader a portion of the text no more extended than can be easily grasped by the eye and by the mind within the space of a few minutes, thus leaving the intelligence of the heart unhampered in its task of spiritual assimilation.

CONTENTS

INTRODUCTION

Here is one of the great spiritual treasures of all time. It is well known among Wayseekers and Wayfarers in the Western world, and well known to be among the great helping resources of the theocentric life.

What is not so well known is the fact that this celebrated small treatise on the path to God is easily misunderstood. Although it is highly esteemed, it is in fact widely underestimated. Its beautiful simplicity overlays, and for a casual reader is apt to conceal, its immense range and depth of meaning.

You will get more out of this book if you are aware of these problems before you start to work with it. The possibilities and difficulties are discussed by one modern commentator* as follows:

Nicholas Herman of Lorraine was a big, clumsy man whose life was turned to God as a result of looking at a tree. Like certain men of Galilee in old times, he was ignorant and uneducated. He was humble enough to enter a monastery, hoping "that he would be made to smart for his awkwardness."

He was admitted as a lay brother among the bare-footed Carmelites in Paris in 1666 and thereafter was known as Brother Lawrence. He was the monastery cook. From the uneventful life of this uncomplicated person there developed, almost by accident, one of the most influential and helpful of all books on the practical search for God.

The Practice of the Presence of God consists of conversations with Brother Lawrence recorded by M. Beaufort, Grand Vicar to the former Cardinal de Noailles, and letters written by Brother Lawrence himself, with no thought that they would ever be published. Emanating from a monastery, these spiritual counsels have been of greatest

* *Invitation to a Great Experiment* by Thomas E. Powers. 1979: Doubleday & Co. Inc.

help to God-seeking men and women in the world.

The practice of the presence of God can be done anywhere by anyone who is not dead, crazy, or asleep. It is direct; it is simple; it involves no theological or intellectual difficulties; it produces genuine spiritual power; it really works. (It does not work as well or as often as it could and should, but that is a curious question which we shall examine below.)

The appeal, the great practical value, and the wide popularity of Brother Lawrence's technique will be found to cut across denominational and interreligious lines. The practice of the presence is praised and studied by Catholics and Protestants alike and has won considerable attention among devoted people outside the Christian tradition.

What is the practice? How do you do it? You can find out by reading the book. But do not be deceived by its simplicity. Do not read it and be charmed by it and put it aside as so many do. Read it slowly, a little bit at a time, daily for six months. And practice it daily. Only by doing it can you begin to know *what* the method is and *how* to do it.

You will notice that the practice of the presence of God consists of three stages. The first is *recollection*. Brother Lawrence teaches us simply to remember—not as philosophy but as living realization in the midst of our ordinary occupations—what is the true state of affairs: God is everywhere. We are continually in his presence. We know this, and yet we do not know it. We alternate between very brief periods of faintly remembering it and very long periods of utterly forgetting it. The practice of the presence begins

with remembering more often and more vividly and forgetting for shorter periods and less completely.

Conversation, like recollection, seems simplicity itself—when you are merely reading about it. When you actually practice it you discover that the simplicity is real all right but that it is a surface beneath which lie a great depth and a great power.

Recollection of the presence and *conversation* with God together represent a critical turning point in the inner life of man. Nearly anyone can remember God and converse with him, now and then. But when you are able to do it more often, and then still more often, a tremendous event is taking place in the soul. This is still a beginner's stage, but it is the *beginning of the true life in God*. Father Reginald Garrigou-Lagrange has written of this experience with wonderful clarity in his synthesis of the spiritual life, *The Three Ages of the Interior Life:*

"As soon as a man ceases to be outwardly occupied, to talk with his fellow men, as soon as he is alone, even in the noisy streets of a great city, he begins to carry on a conversation with himself. If he is young, he often thinks of his future; if he is old, he thinks of the past, and his happy or unhappy experience of life makes him usually judge persons and events very differently.

"If a man is fundamentally egotistical, his intimate conversation with himself is inspired by sensuality or pride. He converses with himself about the object of his cupidity, of his envy; finding therein sadness and death, he tries to flee from himself, to live outside of himself, to divert himself in order to forget the emptiness and the nothingness of his life. In this intimate conversation of the egoist with himself there is a certain very inferior self-knowledge and a no less inferior self-love.

"He is acquainted especially with the sensitive part of his soul, that part which is common to man and to the animal. Thus he has sensible joys, sensible sorrows, according as the weather is pleasant or unpleasant, as he wins money or loses it. He has desires and aversions of the same sensible order; and when he is opposed, he has moments of impatience and anger prompted by inordinate self-love.

"But the egoist knows little about the spiritual part of his soul, that which is common to the angel and to man. Even if he believes in the spirituality of the soul and of the higher faculties, intellect and will, he does not live in this spiritual order. He does not, so to speak, know experimentally this higher part of himself and he does not love it sufficiently. If he knew it, he would find in it the image of God and he would begin to love himself, not in an egotistical manner for himself, but for God. His thoughts almost always fall back on what is inferior in him, and though he often shows intelligence and cleverness which may even become craftiness and cunning, his intellect, instead of rising, always inclines toward what is inferior to it. . . . The intimate conversation of the egoist with himself proceeds thus to death and is therefore not an interior life. . . . The interior life is precisely an elevation and a transformation of the intimate conversation that everyone has with himself as soon as it tends to become a conversation with God."

(1) Recollection of God and (2) conversation with God, as taught in the simple, uncomplicated, authoritative terms of Brother Lawrence, rep-

resent an outlook and a technique which lead to the third and culminating stage of the practice of the presence, the condition of (3) sustained awareness.

When you reach this point, your own efforts become so blended with the grace of God that you who once had to swim so hard now find yourself drifting with the current of God's love, and you who tried with such difficulty to walk toward God now find yourself upheld and carried, constantly, steadily, by an ever present Power. Knowledge of God and communion with God in the stage of sustained awareness are spontaneous, effortless, and rarely interrupted. The presence is known and communed with under all kinds of circumstances.

But if the practice of the presence of God is so easy and so effective, why is it that more people do not follow it through to the stage of sustained awareness as Brother Lawrence himself did? *As a matter of actual fact, not many do.* But why don't they?

Getting down to contemporary cases, here is what we find: The practice of the presence *is* easy to try. Let's say you are one of the many people who try it, and you find to your delight that in a few days you are making undoubted and exhilarating progress. And then . . . then . . . several months later you wake up and find that somehow, somewhere, you have dropped it completely and forgotten all about it. It is not consciously abandoned. No decision is made. The great adventure simply peters out, and you cannot tell for sure just where the stream disappeared in the desert.

But you are intrigued. You remember the joy of those few days when it was working so wonderfully and so easily. So you try it again. And again it works very well! You are thrilled. You resolve to be more alert and not to lose it again. Days go by, great days. And then . . . then . . . the strange drama is repeated. You come to, and you realize that you have not been practicing the presence of God for weeks.

Some good comes from these sporadic and unsustained experiences in Brother Lawrence's technique. But the fact remains that they fall far short of the thing Brother Lawrence is talking about, and they are distressingly in the majority.

Why?

First, probably because the ease and simplicity of the practice of the presence are only part of the picture. The practice is a long ladder. Its feet are comfortably planted at the easy levels where all may climb. But the upper rungs rise into clouds of glory. As the apostles did at the transfiguration, you are apt to fall asleep in this rarefied atmosphere; and then you fall off the ladder.

The great quality, therefore, in practicing the presence is the persistence to try again and again. Do not be discouraged when, time after time, you undergo the humiliating experience of falling asleep spiritually and simply forgetting that God is here and that we may converse with him always. This kind of sleep lies close to the root of the fall of man; it is embarrassing, but the difficulty is made bearable by the realization that you share it with the rest of the human race.

Anyone who wishes seriously to study and practice Brother Lawrence's way should read Gerald Heard's two essays on the subject, entitled "Notes on Brother Lawrence's Practice," in *Vedanta for the Western World*. With his combination of scholarship and spiritual insight,

Heard shows that there is much more than meets the casual glance in *The Practice of the Presence of God*. Without wishing to detract from the appeal and comfort and usefulness of the book, he points out that it can be understood and successfully followed only after penetrating study of its content and meditation upon its real meaning.

". . . That method [the practice of the presence], though the description of it has been popular, has owed its popularity not to the fact that it is really simple or rudimentary but because we have felt sentimental about a pretty title and a charming old man. . . ."

"The first thing that a careful study of these four conversations and fifteen letters discloses is that though the language is so simple, often even conventional, yet they contain far more specific information than the easy rapid reading suggests . . . . We find that this is not at all a beginner's book. . . . The system is simple because it is advanced. This is not a spiritual child speaking with unreflective simplicity. This is a man at the end of an intense, never-remitted struggle of a dedicated lifetime, having won to that consummate ease, that master's power to extemporize in any mode, which comes only to those who, at the top and climax of their form, having achieved all particular controls, now have such perfect command of expression and apprehension that every event becomes precisely that opportunity which allows fresh, unexhaustible creativeness to be exhibited."*

Who is right—those who see in Brother Law-

* "Notes on Brother Lawrence" by Gerald Heard in *Vedanta for the Western World*, Christopher Isherwood, Ed. 1945: The Marcel Rodd Co., Hollywood, California.

rence and his way a direct, unconfused, and wonderfully easy method of living the practical life in God, or Gerald Heard, who sees in Lawrence a man very far advanced in sanctity and in his practice an expert's, not a novice's, technique?

Both views may be true. So many ordinary people have been attracted to the practice of the presence and greatly helped by it that we must agree with the enthusiasts who praise it as one of the great and basic spiritual practices. At the same time, so many give up serious attempts really to follow it after a few trials that we must also conclude that Gerald Heard is to be thanked for reminding us that the simplicity of this attractive, easy-to-try practice hides a master's way to the highest perfection.

For this very reason, however—just *because* it combines comfort and encouragement for the beginner with the scope and scale of deepest spirituality—it is a peculiar treasure of counsel in the quest for God. Let no one be put off by the paradoxical extremes of its range. Let the beginner be fed by its simplicity and clarity. And let the more mature seeker drink of its hidden springs. And let them respect and honor each other, so that the one will not be embarrassed by his novice's position or the other inflated by his own progress.

For the average person just starting out on the living of the life in God, Brother Lawrence's practice is a thoroughly sound guide, a perfectly possible and practical method to follow, containing a built-in challenge and test of his sincerity and his capacity to keep going when the practice would lead him into really deep awareness of the presence.

Part I

THE CONVERSATIONS

THE FIRST CONVERSATION

The first time I saw Brother Lawrence was upon the third of August, 1666. He told me that God had done him a singular favor in his conversion at the age of eighteen.

That in the winter, seeing a tree stripped of its leaves, and considering that within a little time the leaves would be renewed, and after that the flowers and fruit appear, he received a high view of the providence and power of

God, which has never since been effaced from his soul. That this view had perfectly set him loose from the world, and kindled in him such a love for God that he could not tell whether it had increased during the more than forty years he had lived since.

That he had been footman to M. Fieubert, the treasurer, and that he was a great awkward fellow who broke everything.

That he had desired to be received into a monastery, thinking that he would there be made to smart for his awkwardness and the faults he should commit, and so he should sacrifice to God his life, with its pleasures; but that God had disappointed him, he having met with nothing but satisfaction in that state.

That we should establish ourselves in a sense of God's presence by continually conversing with Him. That it was a

shameful thing to quit His conversation to think of trifles and fooleries.

That we should feed and nourish our souls with high notions of God; which would yield us great joy in being devoted to Him.

That we ought to quicken—i.e., to enliven—our faith. That it was lamentable we had so little; and that instead of taking *faith* for the rule of their conduct, men amused themselves with trivial devotions, which changed daily. That the way of faith was the spirit of the church, and that it was sufficient to bring us to a high degree of perfection.

That we ought to give ourselves up to God, with regard both to things temporal and spiritual, and seek our satisfaction only in the fulfilling of

His will, whether He lead us by suffering or by consolation, for all would be equal to a soul truly resigned. That we needed fidelity in those drynesses or insensibilities and irksomenesses in prayer by which God tries our love for Him; that *then* was the time for us to make good and effectual acts of resignation, whereof one alone would oftentimes very much promote our spiritual advancement.

That as for the miseries and sins he heard of daily in the world, he was so far from wondering at them that, on the contrary, he was surprised that there were not more, considering the malice sinners were capable of; that, for his part, he prayed for them; but knowing that God could remedy the mischiefs they did when He pleased, he gave himself no further trouble.

That to arrive at such resignation as

God requires, we should watch atten-
tively over all the passions which mingle
as well in spiritual things as in those of a
grosser nature; that God would give light
concerning those passions to those who
truly desire to serve Him. That if this
was my design, viz., sincerely to serve
God, I might come to him (Brother Lawrence) as often as I pleased, without any
fear of being troublesome; but if not,
that I ought no more to visit him.

THE SECOND CONVERSATION

That he had always been governed by love, without selfish views; and that having resolved to make the love of God the *end* of all his actions, he had found reasons to be well satisfied with his method. That he was pleased when he could take up a straw from the ground for the love of God, seeking Him only, and nothing else, not even His gifts.

That he had been long troubled in

mind from a certain belief that he should be damned; that all the men in the world could not have persuaded him to the contrary; but that he had thus reasoned with himself about it: *I engaged in a religious life only for the love of God and I have endeavored to act only for Him; whatever becomes of me, whether I be lost or saved, I will always continue to act purely for the love of God I shall have this good at least, that till death I shall have done all that is in me to love Him.* That this trouble of mind lasted four years, during which time he had suffered much; but that at last he had seen that this trouble arose from want of faith, and that since then he had passed his life in perfect liberty and continual joy. That he had placed his sins betwixt him and God, as it were, to tell Him that he did not deserve His favors, but that God still continued to

bestow them in abundance.

That in order to form a habit of conversing with God continually, and referring all we do to Him, we must at first apply to Him with some diligence; but that after a little care we should find His love inwardly excite us to it without any difficulty.

That he expected, after the pleasant days God had given him, he should have his turn of pain and suffering; but that he was not uneasy about it, knowing very well that as he could do nothing of himself, God would not fail to give him the strength to bear it.

That when an occasion of practicing some virtue offered, he addressed himself to God, saying, *Lord, I cannot do*

this unless Thou enablest me; and that then he received strength more than sufficient.

That when he had failed in his duty, he only confessed his fault, saying to God, *I shall never do otherwise if You leave me to myself; it is You who must hinder my falling and mend what is amiss.* That after this he gave himself no further uneasiness about it.

That we ought to act with God in the greatest simplicity, speaking to Him frankly and plainly, and imploring His assistance in our affairs, just as they happen. That God never failed to grant it, as he had often experienced.

That he had been lately into Burgundy, to buy the provision of wine for the society, which was a very unwelcome task for him, because he had no turn for business, and because he was lame and could not go about the boat but by rolling himself over the casks. That, however, he gave himself no uneasiness about it, nor about the purchase of the wine. That he said to God, *It was His business he was about*, and that he afterward found it very well performed. That he had been sent into Auvergne, the year before, upon the same account; that he could not tell how the matter passed, but that it proved very well.

So, likewise, in his business in the kitchen (to which he had naturally a great aversion), having accustomed himself to do everything there for the love of God, and with prayer, upon all occasions, for His grace to do his work well, he had found everything easy, during

fifteen years that he had been employed there.

That he was very well pleased with the post he was now in; but that he was as ready to quit that as the former, since he was always pleasing himself in every condition by doing little things for the love of God.

That with him the set times of prayer were not different from other times; that he retired to pray, according to the directions of his superior, but that he did not want such retirement, nor ask for it, because his greatest business did not divert him from God.

That as he knew his obligation to love God in all things, and as he endeavored so to do, he had no need of a director to advise him, but that he needed much a confessor to absolve him. That he was very sensible of his faults, but not discouraged by them; that he confessed

them to God, but did not plead against Him to excuse them. When he had so done, he peaceably resumed his usual practice of love and adoration.

That in his trouble of mind he had consulted nobody, but knowing only by the light of faith that God was present, he contented himself with directing all his actions to Him, i.e., doing them with a desire to please Him, let what would come of it.

That useless thoughts spoil all; that the mischief began there; but that we ought to reject them as soon as we perceived their impertinence to the matter in hand, or our salvation, and return to our communion with God.

That at the beginning he had often passed his time appointed for prayer in

rejecting wandering thoughts and falling back into them. That he could never regulate his devotion by certain methods as some do. That, nevertheless, at first he had *meditated* for some time, but afterward that went off, in a manner he could give no account of.

That all bodily mortifications and other exercises are useless, except as they serve to arrive at the union with God by love; that he had well considered this, and found it the shortest way to go straight to Him by a continual exercise of love and doing all things for His sake.

That we ought to make a great difference between the acts of the *understanding* and those of the *will*; that the first were comparatively of little value, and the others, all. That our only business was to love and delight ourselves in God.

That all possible kinds of mortification, if they were void of the love of God, could not efface a single sin. That we ought, without anxiety, to expect the pardon of our sins from the blood of Jesus Christ, only endeavoring to love Him with all our hearts. That God seemed to have granted the greatest favors to the greatest sinners, as more signal monuments of His mercy.

That the greatest pains or pleasures of this world were not to be compared with what he had experienced of both kinds in a spiritual state; so that he was careful for nothing and feared nothing, desiring only one thing of God, namely, that he might not offend Him.

That he had no scruples; for, said he, when I fail in my duty, I readily ac-

knowledge it, saying, I am used to do so; I shall never do otherwise if I am left to myself. If I fail not, then I give God thanks, acknowledging that the strength comes from Him.

THE THIRD CONVERSATION

He told me that the *foundation of the spiritual life* in him had been a high notion and esteem of God in faith; which when he had once well conceived, he had no other care at first but faithfully to reject every other thought, *that he might perform all his actions for the love of God*. That when sometimes he had not thought of God for a good while, he did not disquiet himself for it; but, after having acknowl-

edged his wretchedness to God, he returned to Him with so much the greater trust in Him as he had found himself wretched through forgetting Him.

That the trust we put in God honors Him much and draws down great graces.

That it was impossible not only that God should deceive, but also that He should long let a soul suffer which is perfectly resigned to Him, and resolved to endure everything for His sake.

That he had so often experienced the ready succor of divine grace upon all occasions, that from the same experience, when he had business to do, he did not think of it beforehand; but when it was time to do it, he found in God, as in a clear mirror, all that was fit for him to do. That of late he had acted thus, without anticipating care; but before the experience above mentioned, he had used it in his affairs.

When outward business diverted him a little from the thought of God, a fresh remembrance coming from God invested his soul, and so inflamed and transported him that it was difficult for him to contain himself.

That he was more united to God in his outward employments than when he left them for devotion and retirement.

That he expected hereafter some great pain of body or mind; that the worst that could happen to him was to lose that sense of God which he had enjoyed so long; but that the goodness of God assured him He would not forsake him utterly, and that He would give him strength to bear whatever evil He permitted to happen to him; and therefore

that he feared nothing, and had no occasion to consult with anybody about his state. That when he had attempted to do it, he had always come away more perplexed; and that as he was conscious of his readiness to lay down his life for the love of God, he had no apprehension of danger. That perfect resignation to God was a sure way to heaven, a way in which we had always sufficient light for our conduct.

That in the beginning of the spiritual life we ought to be faithful in doing our duty and denying ourselves; but after that, unspeakable pleasures followed. That in difficulties we need only have recourse to Jesus Christ, and beg His grace; with that everything became easy.

That many do not advance in the Christian progress because they stick in penances and particular exercises, while

they neglect the love of God, which is the *end*. That this appeared plainly by their works, and was the reason why we see so little solid virtue.

That there needed neither art nor science for going to God, but only a heart resolutely determined to apply itself to nothing but Him, or for His sake, and to love Him only.

THE FOURTH CONVERSATION

He talked with me very frequently, and with great openness of heart, concerning his manner of going to God, whereof some part is related already.

He told me that all consists *in one hearty renunciation* of everything which we are sensible does not lead to God. That we might accustom ourselves to a continual conversation with Him, with freedom and in simplicity. That we need

only to recognize God intimately present with us, to address ourselves to Him every moment, that we may beg His assistance for knowing His will in things doubtful, and for rightly performing those which we plainly see He requires of us, offering them to Him before we do them, and giving Him thanks when we have done.

That in this conversation with God we are also employed in praising, adoring, and loving Him incessantly, for His infinite goodness and perfection.

That, without being discouraged on account of our sins, we should pray for His grace with a perfect confidence, as relying upon the infinite merits of our Lord Jesus Christ. That God never failed offering us His grace at each action; that he distinctly perceived it, and never failed of it, unless when his thoughts had wandered from a sense of God's presence, or he had forgotten to ask His assistance.

That God always gave us light in our doubts when we had no other design but to please Him.

That our sanctification did not depend upon *changing* our works, but in doing that for God's sake which we commonly do for our own. That it was lamentable to see how many people mistook the means for the end, addicting themselves to certain works, which they performed very imperfectly, by reason of their human or selfish regards.

That the most excellent method he had found of going to God was that of doing our common business without any view of pleasing men, and (as far as we are capable)

purely for the love of God.*

That it was a great delusion to think that the times of prayer ought to differ from other times; that we are as strictly obliged to adhere to God by action in the time of action as by prayer in the season of prayer.

That his prayer was nothing else but a sense of the presence of God, his soul being at that time insensible to everything but divine love; and that when the appointed times of prayer were past, he found no difference, because he still continued with God, praising and blessing Him with all his might, so that he passed his life in continual joy; yet hoped that God would give him somewhat to suffer when he should grow stronger.

That we ought, once for all, heartily

* Gal 1:10, Eph. 6:5,6.

to put our whole trust in God, and make a total surrender of ourselves to Him, secure that He would not deceive us.

That we ought not to be weary of doing little things for the love of God, who regards not the greatness of the work, but the love with which it is performed. That we should not wonder if, in the beginning, we often failed in our endeavors, but that at last we should gain a habit, which will naturally produce its acts in us, without our care, and to our exceeding great delight.

That the whole substance of religion was faith, hope, and charity, by the practice of which we become united to the will of God; that all besides is indifferent, and to be used as a means that

we may arrive at our end, and be swallowed up therein, by faith and charity.

That all things are possible to him who *believes;* that they are less difficult to him who *hopes;* that they are more easy to him who *loves,* and still more easy to him who perseveres in the practice of these three virtues.

That the end we ought to propose to ourselves is to become, in this life, the most perfect worshippers of God we can possibly be, as we hope to be through all eternity.

That when we enter upon the spiritual life, we should consider and examine to the bottom what we are. And then we should find ourselves worthy of all contempt, and not deserving indeed the name of Christians; subject to all kinds of misery and numberless accidents, which trouble us and cause perpetual vicissitudes in our health, in our humors, in our internal and external dispositions; in fine, persons whom God would humble by many pains and labors, as well within as without. After this we should not wonder that troubles, temptations, oppositions, and contradictions happen to us from men. We ought, on the contrary, to submit ourselves to them, and bear them as long as God pleases, as things highly advantageous to us.

That the greater perfection a soul aspires after, the more dependent it is upon divine grace.*

Being questioned by one of his own society (to whom he was obliged to open himself) by what means he had attained such an habitual sense of God, he

* The particulars which follow are collected from other accounts of Brother Lawrence.

told him that, since his first coming to the monastery, he had considered God as the end of all his thoughts and desires, as the mark to which they should tend, and in which they should terminate.

That in the beginning of his novitiate he spent the hours appointed for private prayer in thinking of God, so as to convince his mind of, and to impress deeply upon his heart, the divine existence, rather by devout sentiments, and submission to the lights of faith, than by studied reasonings and elaborate meditations. That by this short and sure method he exercised himself in the knowledge and love of God, resolving to use his utmost endeavor to live in a continual sense of His presence, and, if possible, never to forget Him more.

That when he had thus in prayer filled his mind with great sentiments of that

infinite Being, he went to his work appointed in the kitchen (for he was cook to the society). There having first considered severally the things his office required, and when and how each thing was to be done, he spent all the intervals of his time, as well before as after his work, in prayer.

That when he began his business, he said to God, with a filial trust in Him: *O my God, since Thou art with me, and I must now, in obedience to Thy commands, apply my mind to these outward things, I beseech Thee to grant me the grace to continue in Thy presence; and to this end do Thou prosper me with Thy assistance, receive all my works, and possess all my affections.*
As he proceeded in his work he con-

tinued his familiar conversation with his Maker, imploring His grace, and offering to Him all his actions.

When he had finished he examined himself how he had discharged his duty; if he found *well*, he returned thanks to God; if otherwise, he asked pardon, and, without being discouraged, he set his mind right again, and continued his exercise of the *presence* of God as if he had never deviated from it. "Thus," said he, "by rising after my falls, and by frequently renewed acts of faith and love, I am come to a state wherein it would be as difficult for me not to think of God as it was at first to accustom myself to it."

As Brother Lawrence had found such an advantage in walking in the presence of God, it was natural for him to recommend it earnestly to others; but his example was a stronger inducement than any arguments he could propose. His very countenance was edifying, such a sweet and calm devotion appearing in it as could not but affect the beholders. And it was observed that in the greatest hurry of business in the kitchen he still preserved his recollection and heavenly mindedness. He was never hasty nor loitering, but did each thing in its season, with an even, uninterrupted composure and tranquillity of spirit. "The time of business," said he, "does not with me differ from the time of prayer, and in the noise and clatter of my kitchen, while several persons are at the same time calling for different things, I possess God in as great tranquillity as if I were upon my knees at the blessed sacrament."

Part II

THE LETTERS

THE FIRST LETTER

Since you desire so earnestly that I should communicate to you the method by which I arrived at that *habitual sense of God's presence,* which our Lord, of His mercy, has been pleased to vouchsafe to me, I must tell you that it is with great difficulty that I am prevailed on by your importunities; and now I do it only upon the terms that you show my letter to nobody. If I knew that you would let it be seen, all the de-

sire that I have for your advancement would not be able to determine me to it. The account I can give you is:

Having found in many books different methods of going to God, and divers practices of the spiritual life, I thought this would serve rather to puzzle me than facilitate what I sought after, which was nothing but how to become wholly God's. This made me resolve to give the all for the all; so after having given myself wholly to God, that He might take away my sin, *I renounced, for the love of Him, everything that was not He, and I began to live as if there was none but He and I in the world.* Sometimes I considered myself before Him as a poor criminal at the feet of his judge; at other times I beheld Him in my heart as my Father, as my God. I worshipped him the oftenest that I could, keeping my mind in His holy presence, and recalling it as often as I found it wandered from Him.

I found no small pain in this exercise, and yet I continued it, notwithstanding all the difficulties that occurred, without troubling or disquieting myself when my mind had wandered involuntarily. I made this my business as much all the day long as at the appointed times of prayer; for at all times, every hour, every minute, even in the height of my business, I drove away from my mind everything that was capable of interrupting my thought of God.

Such has been my common practice ever since I entered in religion; and though I have done it very imperfectly, yet I have found great advantages by it. These, I well know, are

to be imputed to the mere mercy and goodness of God, because we can do nothing without Him, and *I* still less than any. But when we are faithful to keep ourselves in His holy presence, and set Him always before us, this not only hinders our offending Him and doing anything that may displease Him, at least willfully, but it also begets in us a holy freedom, and if I may so speak, a familiarity with God, wherewith we ask, and that successfully, the graces we stand in need of. In fine, by often repeating these acts, they become *habitual,* and the presence of God rendered as it were *natural* to us. Give Him thanks, if you please, with me, for His great goodness toward me, which I can never sufficiently admire, for the many favors He has done to so miserable a sinner as I am. May all things praise Him. Amen.

THE SECOND LETTER

Not finding my manner of life in books, although I have no difficulty about it, yet, for greater security, I shall to be glad to know your thoughts concerning it.

In a conversation some days since with a person of piety, he told me the spiritual life was a life of grace, which begins with servile fear, which is increased by hope of eternal life, and which is consummated by pure love;

that each of these states had its different stages, by which one arrives at last at that blessed consummation.

I have not followed all these methods. On the contrary, from I know not what instincts, I found they discouraged me. This was the reason why, at my entrance into religion, I took a resolution to give myself up to God, as the best return I could make for His love, and, for the love of Him, to renounce all besides.

For the first year I commonly employed myself during the time set apart for devotion with the thought of death, judgment, heaven, hell, and my sins. Thus I continued some years, applying my mind carefully the rest of the day, and even in the midst of my business, *to the presence of God,* whom I considered always as *with* me, often as *in* me.

At length I came insensibly to do the same thing during my set time of prayer, which caused in me great delight and consolation. This practice produced in me so high an esteem for God that *faith* alone was capable to satisfy me in that point.*

Such was my beginning, and yet I must tell you that for the first ten years I suffered much. The apprehension that I was not devoted to God as I wished to be, my past sins always present to my

---

* I suppose he means that all distinct notions he could form of God were unsatisfactory, because he perceived them to be unworthy of God; and therefore his mind was not to be satisfied but by the views of *faith*, which apprehend God as infinite and incomprehensible, as He is in Himself, and not as He can be conceived by human ideas. —M. Beaufort

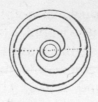

mind, and the great unmerited favors
which God did me, were the matter and
source of my sufferings. During this time
I fell often, and rose again presently. It
seemed to me that all creatures, reason,
and God Himself were against me, and
faith alone for me. I was troubled sometimes with thoughts that to believe I had
received such favors was an effect of my
presumption, which pretended to be *at
once* where others arrive with difficulty;
at other times, that it was a willful delusion, and that there was no salvation for
me.

When I thought of nothing but to end
my days in these troubles (which did not
at all diminish the trust I had in God,
and which served only to increase my
faith), I found myself changed all at
once; and my soul, which till that time
was in trouble, felt a profound inward
peace, as if she were in her center and

place of rest.

Ever since that time I walk before God simply, in faith, with humility and with love, and I apply myself diligently to do nothing and think nothing which may displease Him. I hope that when I have done what I can, He will do with me what He pleases.

As for what passes at present, I cannot express it. I have no pain or difficulty about my state, because I have no will but that of God, which I endeavor to accomplish in all things, and to which I am so resigned that I would not take up a straw from the ground against His order, or from any other motive than purely that of love to Him.

I have quitted all forms of devotion

and set prayers but those to which my state obliges me. And I make it my business only to persevere in His holy presence, wherein I keep myself by a simple attention, and a general fond regard to God, which I may call an *actual presence* of God; or, to speak better, an habitual, silent, and secret conversation of the soul with God, which often causes me joys and raptures inwardly, and sometimes also outwardly, so great that I am forced to use means to moderate them and prevent their appearance to others.

In short, I am assured beyond all doubt that my soul has been with God above these thirty years. I pass over many things that I may not be tedious to you, yet I think it proper to inform you after what manner I consider myself before God, whom I behold as my King.

I consider myself as the most wretched of men, full of sores and corruption, and who has committed all sorts of crimes against his King. Touched with a sensible regret, I confess to Him all my wickedness, I ask His forgiveness, I abandon myself in His hands that He may do what He pleases with me. The King, full of mercy and goodness, very far from chastising me, embraces me with love, makes me eat at His table, serves me with His own hands, gives me the key of His treasures; He converses and delights Himself with me incessantly, in a thousand and a thousand ways, and treats me in all respects as His favorite. It is thus I consider myself from time to time in His holy presence.

My most useful method is this simple attention, and such a general passionate

regard to God, to whom I find myself often attached with greater sweetness and delight than that of an infant at the mother's breast; so that, if I dare use the expression, I should choose to call this state the bosom of God, for the inexpressible sweetness which I taste and experience there.

If sometimes my thoughts wander from it by necessity or infirmity, I am presently recalled by inward motions so charming and delicious that I am ashamed to mention them. I desire your Reverence to reflect rather upon my great wretchedness, of which you are fully informed, than upon the great favors which God does me, all unworthy and ungrateful as I am.

As for my set hours of prayer, they are only a continuation of the same exercise. Sometimes I consider myself there as a stone before a carver, whereof he is to make a statue; presenting myself thus before God, I desire Him to form His perfect image in my soul, and make me entirely like Himself.

At other times, when I apply myself to prayer, I feel all my spirit and all my soul lift itself up without any care or effort of mine, and it continues as it were suspended and firmly fixed in God, as in its center and place of rest.

I know that some charge this state with inactivity, delusion, and self-love. I confess that it is a holy inactivity, and would be a happy self-love if the soul in that state were capable of it, because, in effect, while she is in this repose, she cannot be disturbed by such acts as she was formerly accustomed to, and which were then her

support, but which would now rather hinder than assist her.

Yet I cannot bear that this should be called delusion, because the soul which thus enjoys God desires herein nothing but Him. If this be delusion in me, it belongs to God to remedy it. Let Him do what He pleases with me; I desire only Him, and to be wholly devoted to Him. You will, however, oblige me in sending me your opinion, to which I always pay a great deference, for I have a singular esteem for your Reverence.

THE THIRD LETTER

We have a God who is infinitely gracious and knows all our wants. I always thought that He would reduce you to extremity. He will come in His own time, and when you least expect it. Hope in Him more than ever; thank Him with me for the favors He does you, particularly for the fortitude and patience which He gives you in your afflictions. It is a plain mark of the care He takes of you. Comfort yourself, then,

with Him, and give thanks for all.

I admire also the fortitude and bravery of Mr. ——. God has given him a good disposition and a good will; but there is in him still a little of the world and a great deal of youth. I hope the affliction which God has sent him will prove a wholesome remedy to him, and make him enter into himself. It is an accident which should engage him to put all his trust in Him who accompanies him everywhere. Let him think of Him as often as he can, especially in the greatest dangers. A little lifting up of the heart suffices. A little remembrance of God, one act of inward worship, though upon a march, and a sword in hand, are prayers, which, however short, are nevertheless very acceptable to God; and far from lessening a soldier's courage in occasions of danger, they best serve to fortify it.

Let him then think of God the most he can. Let him accustom himself, by degrees, to this small but holy exercise. No one will notice it, and nothing is easier than to repeat often in the day these little internal adorations. Recommend to him, if you please, that he think of God the most he can, in the manner here directed. It is very fit and most necessary for a soldier who is daily exposed to the dangers of life. I hope that God will assist him and all the family, to whom I present my service.

THE FOURTH LETTER

I have taken this opportunity to communicate to you the sentiments of one of our society, concerning the admirable effects and continual assistances which he receives from the *presence of God*. Let you and me both profit by them.

You must know his continual care has been, for about forty years past that he has spent in religion, to be *always with God,* and to do nothing, say nothing, and think nothing which may displease Him, and this without any other view than purely for the love of Him, and because He deserves infinitely more.

He is now so accustomed to that *divine presence* that he receives from it continual succor upon all occasions. For about thirty years his soul has been filled with joys so continual, and sometimes so great, that he is forced to use means to moderate them, and to hinder their appearing outwardly.

If sometimes he is a little too much absent from that *divine presence,* God presently makes Himself to be felt in his soul to recall him, which often happens when he is most engaged in his outward business. He answers with exact fidelity to these inward drawings,

either by an elevation of his heart toward God, or by a meek and fond regard to Him; or by such words as love forms upon these occasions, as, for instance, *My God, here I am all devoted to Thee. Lord, make me according to Thy heart.* And then it seems to him (as in effect he feels it) that this God of love, satisfied with such few words, reposes again, and rests in the fund and center of his soul. The experiences of these things gives him such an assurance that God is always in the fund or bottom of his soul that it renders him incapable of doubting it upon any account whatever.

Judge by this what content and satisfaction he enjoys while he continually finds in himself so great a treasure. He is no longer in an anxious search after it, but has it open before him, and may take what he pleases of it.

He complains much of our blindness,

and cries often that we are to be pitied who content ourselves with so little. *God*, saith he, *has infinite treasure to bestow, and we take up with a little sensible devotion, which passes in a moment. Blind as we are, we hinder God and stop the current of His graces. But when He finds a soul penetrated with a lively faith, He pours into it His graces and favors plentifully; there they flow like a torrent which, after being forcibly stopped against its ordinary course, when it has found a passage, spreads itself with impetuosity and abundance.*

Yes, we often stop this torrent by the little value we set upon it. But let us stop it no more; let us enter into ourselves and break down the bank which hinders it. Let us make way for grace; let us redeem the lost time, for perhaps we have but little left. Death follows us close; let us be well prepared for it; for we die but once, and a miscarriage *there* is irretrievable.

I say again, let us enter into ourselves. The time presses, there is no room for delay; our souls are at stake. I believe you have taken such effectual measures that you will not be surprised. I commend you for it; it is the one thing necessary. We must, nevertheless, always work at it, because not to advance in the spiritual life is to go back. But those who have the gale of the Holy Spirit go forward even in sleep. If the vessel of our soul is still tossed with winds and storms, let us awake the Lord, who reposes in it, and He will quickly calm the sea.

I have taken the liberty to impart to you these good sentiments, that you

may compare them with your own. It will serve again to kindle and inflame them, if by misfortune (which God forbid, for it would be indeed a great misfortune) they should be, though never so little, cooled. Let us then *both* recall our first fervors. Let us profit by the example and the sentiments of this brother, who is little known of the world, but known of God, and extremely caressed by Him. I will pray for you; do you pray instantly for me.

THE FIFTH LETTER

I received this day two books and a letter from Sister ——, who is preparing to make her profession, and upon that account desires the prayers of your holy society, and yours in particular. I perceive that she reckons much upon them; pray do not disappoint her. Beg of God that she may make her sacrifice in the view of His love alone, and with a firm resolution to be wholly devoted to Him. I will send you one of these books, which treat of *the presence of God,* a subject which, in my opinion, contains the whole spiritual life; and it seems to me that whoever duly practices it will soon become spiritual.

I know that for the right practice of it the heart must be empty of all other things, because God will possess the heart *alone;* and as He cannot possess it *alone* without emptying it of all besides, so neither can He act *there,* and do in it what He pleases, unless it be left vacant to Him.

There is not in the world a kind of life more sweet and delightful than that of a continual conversation with God. Those only can comprehend it who practice and experience it; yet I do not advise you to do it from that motive. It is not pleasure which we ought to seek in this exercise; but let us do it from a principle

of love, and because God would have us.

Were I a preacher, I should, above all other things, preach the practice of *the presence of God;* and were I a director, I should advise all the world to do it, so necessary do I think it, and so easy, too.

Ah! if we but knew the want we have of the grace and assistance of God, we should never lose sight of Him—no, not for a moment. Believe me; make immediately a holy and firm resolution nevermore willfully to forget Him, and to spend the rest of your days in His sacred presence, deprived, for the love of Him, if He thinks fit, of all consolations.

Set heartily about this work, and if you do it as you ought, be assured that you will soon find the effects of it. I will assist you with my prayers, poor as they are. I recommend myself earnestly to yours and those of your holy society.

THE SIXTH LETTER

I have received from Mrs. —— the things which you gave her for me. I wonder that you have not given me your thoughts of the little book I sent to you, and which you have received. Pray set heartily about the practice of it in your old age; it is better late than never.

I cannot imagine how religious persons can live satisfied without the practice of the *presence of God*. For my part, I keep myself retired with Him in the fund or center of my soul as much as I can; and while I am so with Him I fear nothing, but the least turning from Him is insupportable.

This exercise does not much fatigue the body; it is, however, proper to deprive it sometimes, nay, often, of many little pleasures which are innocent and lawful, for God will not permit that a soul which desires to be devoted entirely to Him should take other pleasures than with Him: that is more than reasonable.

I do not say that therefore we must put any violent constraint upon ourselves. No, we must serve God in a holy freedom; we must do our business faithfully, without trouble or disquiet, recalling our mind to

God mildly, and with tranquillity, as often as we find it wandering from Him.

It is, however, necessary to put our whole trust in God, laying aside all other cares, and even some particular forms of devotion, though very good in themselves, yet such as one often engages in unreasonably, because these devotions are only means to attain to the end. So when by this exercise of *the presence of God* we are *with Him* who is our end, it is then useless to return to the means; but we may continue with Him our commerce of love, persevering in His holy presence, one while by an act of praise, or adoration, or of desire; one while by an act of resignation or thanksgiving; and in all the ways which our spirit can invent.

Be not discouraged by repugnance which you may find in it from nature; you must do yourself violence. At the first one often thinks it lost time, but you must go on, and resolve to persevere in it to death, notwithstanding all the difficulties that may occur. I recommend myself to the prayers of your holy society, and yours in particular.

THE SEVENTH LETTER

I pity you much. It will be of great importance if you can leave the care of your affairs to ——, and spend the remainder of your life only in worshipping God. He requires no great matters of us: a little remembrance of Him from time to time; a little adoration; sometimes to pray for His grace, sometimes to offer Him your sufferings, and sometimes to return Him thanks for the favors He has given you, and still

gives you, in the midst of your troubles, and to console yourself with Him the oftenest you can. Lift up your heart to Him, sometimes even at your meals, and when you are in company; the least little remembrance will always be acceptable to Him. You need not cry very loud; He is nearer to us than we are aware of.

It is not necessary for being with God to be always at church. We may make an oratory of our heart wherein to retire from time to time to converse with Him in meekness, humility, and love. Everyone is capable of such familiar conversation with God, some more, some less. He knows what we can do. Let us begin, then. Perhaps He expects but one generous resolution on our part. Have courage. We have but little time to live; you are near sixty-four, and I am almost eighty. Let us live and die with God. Sufferings will be sweet and pleasant to us while we are with Him; and the greatest pleasures will be, without Him, a cruel punishment to us. May He be blessed for all. Amen.

Accustom yourself, then, by degrees thus to worship Him, to beg His grace, to offer Him your heart from time to time in the midst of your business, even every moment, if you can. Do not always scrupulously confine yourself to certain rules, or particular forms of devotion, but act with a general confidence in God, with love and humility. You may assure —— of my poor prayers, and that I am their servant.

THE EIGHTH LETTER

You tell me nothing new; you are not the only one that is troubled with wandering thoughts. Our mind is extremely roving; but, as the will is mistress of all our faculties, she must recall them, and carry them to God as their last end.

When the mind, for want of being sufficiently reduced by recollection at our first engaging in devotion, has contracted certain bad habits of wandering and dissipation, they are difficult to over-come, and commonly draw us, even against our wills, to the things of the earth.

I believe one remedy for this is to confess our faults and to humble our-selves before God. I do not advise you to use multiplicity of words in prayer, many words and long discourses being often the occasions of wandering. Hold yourself in prayer before God like a dumb or paralytic beggar at a rich man's gate. Let it be *your* business to keep your mind in the presence of the Lord. If it sometimes wanders and withdraws it-self from Him, do not much disquiet yourself for that: trouble and disquiet serve rather to distract the mind than to recollect it; the will must bring it back in tranquillity. If you persevere in this man-ner, God will have pity on you.

One way to recollect the mind easily

in the time of prayer, and preserve it more in tranquillity, is not to *let it wander too far at other times*. You should keep it strictly in the presence of God; and being accustomed to think of Him often, you will find it easy to keep your mind calm in the time of prayer, or at least to recall it from its wanderings.

I have told you already at large, in my former letters, of the advantages we may draw from this practice of the presence of God. Let us set about it seriously, and pray for one another.

THE NINTH LETTER

The enclosed is an answer to that which I received from ——; pray deliver it to her. She seems to me full of good will, but she would go faster than grace. One does not become holy all at once. I recommend her to you; we ought to help one another by our advice, and yet more by our good examples. You will oblige me to let me hear of her from time to time, and whether she be very fervent and very obedient.

Let us thus think often that our only business in this life is to please God, and that all besides is but folly and vanity. You and I have lived about forty years in religion (i.e., a monastic life). Have we employed them in loving and serving God, who by His mercy has called us to this state, and for that very end? I am filled with shame and confusion when I reflect, on one hand, upon the great favors which God has done, and incessantly continues to do me; and on the other, upon the ill use I have made of them, and my small advancement in the way of perfection.

Since by His mercy He gives us still a little time, let us begin in earnest; let us repair the lost time; let

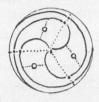

us return with a full assurance to that Father of mercies, who is always ready to receive us affectionately. Let us renounce, let us generously renounce, for the love of Him, all that is not Himself; He deserves infinitely more. Let us put all our trust in Him. I doubt not but we shall soon find the effects of it in receiving the abundance of His grace, with which we can do all things, and without which we can do nothing but sin.

We cannot escape the dangers which abound in life without the actual and continual help of God. Let us, then, pray to Him for it *continually*. How can we pray to Him without being with Him? How can we be with Him but in thinking of Him often? And how can we often think of Him but by a holy habit which we should form of it? You will tell me that I am always saying the same thing. It is true, for this is the best and easiest method I know; and as I use no other, I advise all the world to do it. We must *know* before we can *love*. In order to *know* God, we must often *think* of Him; and when we come to *love* Him, we shall then also think of Him often, for our heart will be with our treasure. This is an argument which well deserves your consideration.

THE TENTH LETTER

I have had a good deal of difficulty to bring myself to write to Mr. ——, and I do it now purely because you and Madam —— desire me. Pray write the directions and send it to him. I am very well pleased with the trust which you have in God; I wish that He may increase it in you more and more. We cannot have too much in so good and faithful a Friend, who will never fail us in this world nor in the next.

If Mr. —— makes his advantage of the loss he has had, and puts all his confidence in God, He will soon give him another friend, more powerful and more inclined to serve him. He disposes of hearts as He pleases. Perhaps Mr. —— was too much attached to him he has lost. We ought to love our friends, but without encroaching upon the love due to God, which must be the principal.

Pray remember what I have recommended to you, which is, to think often on God, by day, by night, in your business, and even in your diversions. He is always near you and with you; leave Him not alone. You would think it rude to leave a friend alone who came to visit you; why, then, must God be neglected? Do not, then, forget Him, but think on Him often, adore Him continually, live and die with Him; this is the glorious

employment of a Christian. In a word, this is our profession; if we do not know it, we must learn it. I will endeavor to help you with my prayers.

THE ELEVENTH LETTER

I do not pray that you may be delivered from your pains, but I pray God earnestly that He would give you strength and patience to bear them as long as He pleases. Comfort yourself with Him who holds you fastened to the cross. He will loose you when He thinks fit. Happy those who suffer with Him. Accustom yourself to suffer in that manner, and seek from Him the strength to endure as much, and as long, as He shall judge to be necessary for you. The men of the world do not comprehend these truths, not is it to be wondered at, since they suffer like what they are, and not like Christians. They consider sickness as a pain to nature, and not as a favor from God; and seeing it only in that light, they find nothing in it but grief and distress. But those who consider sickness as coming from the hand of God, as the effect of His mercy, and the means which He employs for their salvation—such commonly find in it great sweetness and sensible consolation.

I wish you could convince yourself that God is often (in some sense) nearer to us, and more effectually present with us, in sickness than in health. Rely upon no other physician; for, according to my apprehension, He reserves your cure to Himself. Put, then, all your trust in Him, and you will soon find the effects of it in your recovery, which we often retard by putting greater confidence in physic than in God.

Whatever remedies you make use of, they will succeed only so far as He permits. When pains come from God, He only can cure them. He often sends diseases of the body to cure those of the soul. Comfort yourself with the sovereign Physician both of the soul and body.

Be satisfied with the condition in which God places you; however happy you may think me, I envy you. Pains and sufferings would be a paradise to me while I should suffer with my God, and the greatest pleasures would be hell to me if I could relish them without Him. All my consolation would be to suffer something for His sake.

I must, in a little time, go to God. What comforts me in this life is that I now see Him by *faith;* and I see Him in such a manner as might make me say sometimes, *I believe no more, but I see.* I feel what faith teaches us, and in that assurance and that practice of faith I will live and die with Him.

Continue, then, always with God; it is the only support and comfort for your affliction. I shall beseech Him to be with you. I present my service.

THE TWELFTH LETTER

If we were well accustomed to the exercise of the *presence of God,* all bodily diseases would be much alleviated thereby. God often permits that we should suffer a little to purify our souls and oblige us to continue with Him.

Take courage; offer Him your pains incessantly; pray to Him for strength to endure them. Above all, get a habit of entertaining yourself often with God, and forget Him the least you can. Adore Him in your infirmities, offer yourself to Him from time to time, and in the height of your sufferings beseech Him humbly and affectionately (as a child his father) to make you conformable to His holy will. I shall endeavor to assist you with my poor prayers.

God has many ways of drawing us to Himself. He sometimes hides Himself from us; but *faith* alone, which will not fail us in time of need, ought to be our support, and the foundation of our confidence, which must be all in God.

I know not how God will dispose of me. I am always happy. All the world suffers; and I, who deserve the severest discipline, feel joys so continual and so great that I can scarce contain them.

I would willingly ask of God a part of your sufferings, but that I know my weakness, which is so great that if He

left me one moment to myself I should be the most wretched man alive. And yet I know not how He can leave me alone, because faith gives me as strong a conviction as sense can do that He never forsakes us until we have first forsaken Him. Let us live and die in His Presence. Do you pray for me as I for you.

THE THIRTEENTH LETTER

I am in pain to see you suffer so long. What gives me some ease and sweetens the feelings I have for your griefs is that they are proofs of God's love toward you. See them in that view and you will bear them more easily. As your case is, it is my opinion that you should leave off human remedies, and resign yourself entirely to the providence of God. Perhaps He stays only for that resignation and a perfect trust in

Him to cure you. Since, notwithstanding all your cares, physic has hitherto proved unsuccessful, and your malady still increases, it will not be tempting God to abandon yourself in His hands and expect all from Him.

I told you in my last that He sometimes permits bodily diseases to cure the distempers of the soul. Have courage, then; make a virtue of necessity. Ask of God, not deliverance from your pains, but strength to bear resolutely, for the love of Him, all that He should please, and as long as He shall please.

Such prayers, indeed, are a little hard to nature, but most acceptable to God, and sweet to those that love Him. Love sweetens pains; and when one loves God, one suffers for His sake with joy and courage. Do you so, I beseech you; comfort yourself with Him, who is the only Physician of all our maladies. He is

the Father of the afflicted, always ready to help us. He loves us infinitely, more than we imagine. Love Him, then, and seek no consolation elsewhere. I hope you will soon receive it. Adieu. I will help you with my prayers, poor as they are.

THE FOURTEENTH LETTER

I render thanks to our Lord for having relieved you a little, according to your desire. I have been often near expiring, but I never was so much satisfied as then. Accordingly, I did not pray for any relief, but I prayed for strength to suffer with courage, humility, and love. Ah, how sweet it is to suffer with God! However great the sufferings may be, receive them with love. It is paradise to suffer and be with Him;

so that if in this life we would enjoy the peace of paradise we must accustom ourselves to a familiar, humble, affectionate conversation with Him. We must hinder our spirits' wandering from Him upon any occasion. We must make our heart a spiritual temple, wherein to adore Him incessantly. We must watch continually over ourselves, that we may not do nor say nor think anything that may displease Him. When our minds are thus employed about God, suffering will become full of unction and consolation.

I know that to arrive at this state the beginning is very difficult, for we must act purely in faith. But though it is difficult, we know also that we can do all things with the grace of God, which He never refuses to them who ask it earnestly. Knock, persevere in knocking, and I answer for it that He will open to you in His due time, and grant you all at

once what He has deferred during many years. Adieu. Pray to Him for me as I pray to Him for you. I hope to see Him quickly.

THE FIFTEENTH LETTER

God knoweth best what is needful for us, and all that He does is for our good. If we knew how much He loves us, we should always be ready to receive equally and with indifference from His hand the sweet and the bitter. All would please that came from Him. The sorest afflictions never appear intolerable, except when we see them in the wrong light. When we see them as dispensed by the hand of God, when we know that it is our loving Father who abases and distresses us, our sufferings will lose their bitterness and become even matters of consolation.

Let all our employment be to *know* God; the more one *knows* Him, the more one *desires* to know Him. And as *knowledge* is commonly the measure of *love*, the deeper and more extensive our *knowledge* shall be, the greater will be our *love*; and if our love of God were great, we should love Him equally in pains and pleasures.

Let us not content ourselves with loving God for the mere sensible favors, how elevated soever, which He has done or may do us. Such favors, though never so great, cannot bring us so near to Him as faith does in one simple act. Let us seek Him often by faith. He is within us; seek Him not elsewhere. If we do love Him alone, are we not rude, and do we not deserve blame, if we busy ourselves about trifles which do not please and perhaps offend Him? It is to be feared these *trifles* will one day cost us dear.

Let us begin to be devoted to Him in good earnest. Let us cast everything besides out of our hearts. He would possess them alone. Beg this favor of Him. If we do what we can on our parts, we shall soon see that change wrought in us which we aspire after. I cannot thank Him sufficiently for the relaxation He has vouchsafed you. I hope from His mercy the favor to see Him within a few days.* Let us pray for one another.

---

* He took to his bed two days after, and died within the week.

The Upstate Group of All Addicts Anonymous
P.O. Box 500
Hankins, NY 12741
Phone: 1-888-4 AAA GROUP
(1-888-422-2476)
Web: www.alladdictsanonymous.org

THE LIFESAVERS
PROGRAM

Practicing the ethical and
spiritual principles common
to all mankind

A lifesaver, in our view, is anyone who is practicing some or all of the lifesavers principles, effectively and honestly, to stay spiritually alive. By this definition, of course, the world is full of lifesavers and lifesavers groups.

The lifesavers program, as we understand it, is an epitome of basic life-changing principles common to the great spiritual Traditions of mankind. These age-less principles have been wrought into various brief, practical formulae in the crucible of modern experi-ence over the past 150 years. The following are state-ments of lifesavers principles as practiced in effective lifesavers groups in our critical times:

The Seven Common Denominators: Core principles which are common to most lifesavers groups. Very simple but very fundamental, very deep, and very powerful:

1. Realization of need
2. Allegiance to the truth
3. Awakening of faith
4. Surrender to God
5. Commitment to change
6. Cleansing and amendment of life
7. Helping others

The Four Absolutes: Used in the Oxford Group and in the pioneering years of Alcoholics Anonymous, these life-transforming principles in one form or another have been the foundation of the spiritual life in all ages and all cultures. They were the bases, for example, upon which Gandhi's ashram operated; they are among the essentials of the first of the traditional eight limbs of yoga (the *yamas*); and they are clearly the principles to which a life in Christ requires adherence:

1. Absolute honesty—non-lying to oneself or others; fidelity to the truth in thought, word, and actions.
2. Absolute purity—purity of mind, purity of body, purity of the emotions, purity of heart, sexual purity.
3. Absolute unselfishness—seeking what is right and true in every situation above what I want.
4. Absolute love—loving God with all your heart, all your soul, all your mind, and all your strength, and your neighbor as yourself.

The Absolutes of course are not claims of attainment. They are *aims, levels of commitment* for daily conduct. When they are maintained faithfully as *goals*, they become powerful transformers of conduct, character, and consciousness.

The Twelve Steps: One of the most effective and most widely applied statements of the lifesavers principles in modern times, and one of the great working statements of the spiritual life of all times, this fundamental version of the program of Alcoholics Anonymous was in general use throughout the AA Fellowship even before the publication of the "Big Book" (*Alcoholics Anonymous,* AA's basic text) in April 1939. The shorter statements which had preceded it are now forgotten, and the Twelve Steps have become the universally accepted and only generally known version of the AA program.

These steps are a lifeline for alcohol addicts, many of whom, lacking opportunity to contact an AA group, have recovered by the mere knowledge and application of these twelve principles. From the standpoint of the whole world of recovery from addiction, it is impossible to exaggerate the importance of the Twelve Steps of Alcoholics Anonymous. If an addict who is sincerely seeking a way out had no other tool than a working knowledge of these steps, he would have a very good chance of recovery. Do not let the simple language in which they are stated fool you. They are a spiritual powerhouse to which many thousands of alcoholics now walking the streets as free men owe their lives and their liberty.

Adapted versions of the steps have been used by non-alcoholics for many years—by the Al-Anon Family Groups, Neurotics Anonymous, Narcotics Anonymous, Gamblers Anonymous, Overeaters

Anonymous, and many others. The steps as adapted here can be used by anyone. The original version of the steps, for use by alcoholics only, may be found in the Big Book, *Alcoholics Anonymous* (1976: Alcoholics Anonymous World Services, Inc.):

1. We admitted we were powerless, that our lives had become unmanageable.
2. Came to believe that a Power greater than ourselves could restore us to sanity.
3. Made a decision to turn our will and our lives over to the care of God as we understood him.
4. Made a searching and fearless moral inventory of ourselves.
5. Admitted to God, to ourselves, and to another human being the exact nature of our wrongs.
6. Were entirely ready to have God remove all these defects of character.
7. Humbly asked him to remove our shortcomings.
8. Made a list of all persons we had harmed and became willing to make amends to them all.
9. Made direct amends to such people wherever possible, except when to do so would injure them or others.
10. Continued to take personal inventory and when we were wrong promptly admitted it.
11. Sought through prayer and meditation to improve our conscious contact with God as we understood him, praying only for knowledge of his will for us and the power to carry that out.

12. Having had a spiritual awakening as the result of these steps, we tried to carry this message to others, and to practice these principles in all our affairs.

The Ten Practical Points: Chapter five of the book *Alcoholics Anonymous* has always been a faithful guide for people who want to practice the AA program. The following Ten Points are a summary of the life-saving directions given in chapter five, as boiled down and applied by one group of lifesavers. The Ten Points include wisdom of the most practical kind, much of it not found in statements of the AA program outside of chapter five . . .

We commit ourselves to work toward spiritual awakening by sincerely and responsibly trying to do what the AA Big Book suggests:

1. by *completely giving ourselves* to this simple Program;
2. by practicing *rigorous honesty*;
3. by being *willing to go to any lengths* to recover;
4. by being *fearless and thorough* in our practice of the lifesavers principles;
5. by realizing that for us there is *no easier, softer way*;
6. by *letting go of our old ideas absolutely*;
7. by recognizing that *half measures will not work*;
8. by *asking God's protection and care* with complete abandon;
9. by *being willing to grow* along spiritual lines;
10. by accepting the following pertinent ideas as proved by lifesavers experience:
    (a) that *we cannot manage* our own lives;

(b) that probably *no human power can restore us to sanity;*

(c) that *God can and will* if sought.

Altogether (leaving aside the commentaries) there is not a lot of material here. In the entire lifesavers program — the Seven Common Denominators, the Four Absolutes, the Twelve Steps, and the Ten Practical Points—there are only thirty-three things to remember. (In driving an automobile there are four or five times that many.) The lifesavers way of life is based on an astonishingly simple program. *But it embodies the very power of life over death.*

The lifesavers program is a thoroughly tested and proven answer to addiction, but its healing power extends very far beyond that sphere. Our experience proves that *anyone* who is suffering the symptoms of spiritual illness or death—hopelessness, resentment, anxiety, depression, folly, exhaustion—can attain spiritual awakening, self-control, sanity, peace, and joy if he will go to sufficient lengths in adopting these principles as a way of life.

LA